THE HIST(
ANTIQUI
HORSHAM

Howard Dudley

with a new introduction by
Dick Richardson

<small>COUNTRY BOOKS</small>

Published by:
Country Books
Courtyard Cottage, Little Longstone, Bakewell,
Derbyshire DE45 1NN

Tel/Fax: 01629 640670
e-mail: dickrichardson@country-books.co.uk

ISBN 1 898941 72 6

First published 1836 Howard Dudley, London

Printed and bound by:
MFP Design & Print

INTRODUCTION

Howard Dudley was responsible for two of the county's rarest and most desirable topographical books – pure gems for any collector! But who was Howard Dudley, and what was his connection with the old Sussex market town of Horsham?

In the mid-1830s, he wrote and published two small books *Juvenile Researches* (two editions 1835-36) and *The History and Antiquities of Horsham* (1836).

Ignoring the rarity value of these two books, they are nevertheless remarkable because Howard was a schoolboy aged between fourteen and sixteen-years-old when he produced them. He wrote the text, designed the book, typeset it, produced the illustrations by wood engraving and drawing on lithographic stone, printed and bound them. A remarkable feat for one so young!

The printing of different pages is variable, he seems to have experienced problems with inking. On some pages the lines of type resemble an outline of the South Downs through not tying the type securely on the stone – occasionally a character falls below the line. Also, his use of hyphenation can only be described as eccentric.

It must be added that a project of this kind was extremely unusual for a boy still at school (aged 14-16) in the early 19th century. His parents must have been 'comfortably off' for him to be able to invest in a printing press and type.

There seems to be some doubt about the trade his father was in. I suspect, though further research needs to be done, that he was involved in dealing in printing presses and type. The equipment used by his son Howard could well have been secondhand – certainly the battered nature of some of the type would seem to indicate this. George Dudley died in Ghent at the time when the Continent was well known for their type designs and fonts – Aldus Bembo, Garamont, Plantin, etc.

Howard was born in 1820, the only son of a Quaker couple, George and Sarah Dudley, who lived in Salisbury Square, Fleet Street, London. George Dudley was from Tipperary, and his wife, Sarah, was the daughter of Nathaniel Cove, a London coal merchant.

Howard was baptised at the parish church of Shoreditch through the intervention of his nurse, in spite of his parents' Quaker beliefs. Little is known of his father's trade, but he was 'struck down by unknown causes' while in Ghent when Howard was seven years of age.

The untimely death of the father caused the family to leave London and settle at Easebourne, near Midhurst, in West Sussex. It was here that *Juvenile Researches* was first published. This book contains references to Horsham which indicate that he had some knowledge of the town between the years 1828 and 1835. It is more than likely that Howard and his family stayed with Quaker friends in Horsham, though to date, these have not been positively identified.

One possibility is Samuel West who appears in a list of Horsham residents of 1817, listed as gentleman and Quaker living in South Street – now the Causeway. *Juvenile Reseraches* includes a poem entitled *Reflections among the tombs in Horsham Churchyard* by S W—t.

In 1830, a Miss Cove is listed as living near the Carfax – possibly a sister of Howard's mother? In the 1841 census Sarah Cove, aged 65, and Ann Cove, aged 35, both of independent means, are listed as living in Albion Terrace as tenants of Elizabeth Greenfield. Could Sarah Cove have been his grandmother, and Ann, his aunt?

Following the success of *Juvenile Researches,* Howard published *The History and Antiquities of Horsham* in 1836. It is dedicated to The Right Honourable George O'Brien Wyndham, Earl of Egremont – *"the following pages are by his lordship's permission respectfully dedicated by his obliged servant Howard Dudley"*.

At the back of the book it states that it was printed by Howard Dudley in Millbank Street, London, so they seem to have departed from Easbourne by this date. Gas lighting was installed in Horsham in 1836, so Dudley is obviously still up-to-date with events in the town.

It may be that they had moved to London for him to pursue his carrer as a wood engraver. Some years later he issued a prospectus for the publication of *The History and Antiquities of Midhurst and its Vicinity* to contain more than 150 engravings and lithographs. Sadly, this never appeared – probably due to his success as an engraver.

Between 1845 (aged 25) and 1852, he was working in Edinburgh, where he met and married Jane Ellen Young, second daughter of Alexander Young, a painter and glazier. Jane's two younger brothers, Charles and Alexander, were also wood engravers. Howard and Jane were married at St Mary's Catholic Church, Edinburgh, on the 1st December 1849.

Three years later they returned to London and lived at

12 Holford Square, Pentonville, then a highly respectable neighbourhood. Howard died at home of consumption on 4th July, 1864, aged 44. Sadly there were no children to continue the name, but his widow and her two brothers continued the business.

His obituary in the *Gentleman's Magazine* stated *"Mr Dudley was a mild and amiable man, affectionate in his domestic relations, and his gentlemanly manners, bright ideas and pungent remarks, and very great choice of words, made him a delightful companion. He died with an earnest profession of his belief in Jesus Christ."*

* * * * *

I must here record my thanks to my good friend, Tony Wales of Horsham, who made available to me the copy of the book from which this facsimile is produced and also supplied some background on Howard Dudley. I hope that by doing so, I have restored this book to all who love Horsham and Sussex.

Dick Richardson
2002

THE HISTORY AND

ANTIQUITIES OF,

HORSHAM.

By the Author of Juvenile Researches.

ILLUSTRATED BY WOOD ENGRAVINGS

AND LITHOGRAPHIC VIEWS.

LONDON.

1836.

TO THE RT. HON.

GEORGE O'BRIEN WYNDHAM,

Earl of Egremont

AND BARON COCKERMOUTH.

THE FOLLOWING PAGES

ARE BY HIS LORDSHIP'S PERMISSION

RESPECTFULLY DEDICATED

By his obliged servant

Howard Dudley.

ILLUSTRATIONS

LITHOGRAPHIC.

WOOD-CUTS.

HISTORY AND ANTIQUITIES,

OF HORSHAM,

AND ITS VICINITY

The ancient town and borough of Horsham, which has generally been past over in topographical accounts, as a place unworthy of notice; or lost in the dazzling descriptions, of the "modern maritime Babylon of Sussex," must always remain a spot, dear to the lover of antiquities, and romantic scenery. The derivation of its name, has ever continued a matter of great perplexity; which perhaps may be considered as a very strong argument, in favour of the antiquity of the place. Some persons conjecture, that the appellation is derived from the two Saxon words, hurst, and ham, the first syllable signifying a wood, and the second a village or collection of houses : and this opinion seems to be supported by the known fact, that this part of the county, was formerly one entire tract of forest land : but again quite as good if not a superior derivation, may be taken from the two words, Horsa, and ham, that is the village of, or built by, Horsa.

Horsham has enjoyed the privilege of sending two members to Parliament, ever since the year 1295 : by the passing of the reform bill, however, one representative was considered sufficient for the business of the borough. The names of the persons first elected for the town, were Walter Burgeys, and Walter Randolf : Robert Henry Hurst esq. is the present member.

The spring assizes for the county, had also long been held in the Town-Hall of Horsham; but this privilege was selfishly abstracted from the town, by the inhabitants of Lewes; and even the county gaol, which has been stationed here, for time immemorial, is, we understand, to be removed to the all devouring eastern rival : the quarter sessions however, are still held here.

Still, notwithstanding, as respects the town, Horsham is greatly improving : the number of buildings which have been lately erected, and which are still erecting, are of a new and very handsome description : the streets are neatly paved, with the large flat stones procured from the excellent quarries in the neighbourhood ; and the illumination of the streets by gas, which is being carried on with great spirit and energy, contribute very greatly to the general respectability and good appearance of the place.

Horsham consists of 4 principal streets, crossing one another at right angles, with a large square, stretching due N. and S., in the centre. The upper part of this square is commonly denominated the Gaol Green, in consequence of the prison, which formerly stood at the northern end, but of which two large walls, now found useful in an adjacent brewery, only remain.

The lower portion contains the large and handsome Town-Hall, of which the annexed sketch will afford some idea: a few years ago, the appearance which it presented was entirely different, being built on arches, in a similar manner, to the Council chamber, at Chichester, and surmounted by a stone with the inscription "Thirty six miles from Westminster Bridge," engraved thereupon : by the kind liberality of the Duke of Norfolk,

it was completely repaired, and greatly en-
larged ; and though no longer applied to its
original purpose, (except in the instance of
the quarter sessions) it is still found very
serviceable for lectures, public meetings, &c.
&c. The north front is embellished by the
arms of royalty, flanked by those of Norfolk

and Horsham.   On either side of the Hall,
is a neat street, only one of which is a tho-
roughfare ; these meet on the southern side
of the building, in a very handsome and respectable walk, called the Church Causeway,
at the termination of which, is the ancient
and spacious church, (dedicated to St Mary)
the approach is rendered particularly picturesque, by an avenue of lofty lime trees, of
some extent, which leads in a perfectly
straight direction, to the church-yard gateway : the effect of the view from this avenue,
is exceedingly pleasing, particularly of a
summer evening, when the rays of the set-
ting sun cast a beautiful golden tint, upon
the venerable porch, which appears a conspicuous object behind the portal.

   The northern side of the edifice, though
perhaps not quite equal to the southern, appears to great advantage, though the modern
windows, which have been subsituted in several instances for others of great antiquity,

SOUTH VIEW OF HORSHAM CHURCH.

Drawn on Stone by T. Dudley

add greatly to diminish the general effect.

On entering the church by the eastern gateway, the interior of the structure appears to the highest advantage: the large and beautifully simple communion window, reaching

almost from the basement to the roof, is by no means the least attractive object of attention ; while the handsome appearance of the altar, raised by a flight of several steps, covered entirely with crimson cloth ; the unusually large extent of the communion rails and the numerous beautiful monuments, in every direction, afford a very elegant appearance, perhaps not to be equalled by any other parochial edifice in the county. Yet at the same time, the venerable roof of oake planks; the large yet highly sculptured beams which have weathered nearly a thousand years; the tattered escotcheons; the crested helmets; and the antique tombs, afford a view at once pleasing and romantic. ------ Some attempt has been made to illustrate this portion of the church, (the chancel) in the annexed engraving, but no drawing can do justice to the original building.

The dimensions of the church are as below.

Length . . . . 146 ft.
Width . . . . 53 8 in.
Height 47 10

THE CHANCEL

Drawn on Stone by H. Dudley.

THE NAVE.

The roof is supported upon wooden ribs, crossed by others of the same materials: the joints are covered by ornamented plates of iron, of very grotesque descriptions: in the nave, the ribs are almost double the distance apart, of those in the chancel: the junction of the roof and walls, in the latter portion of the edifice, are adorned with curious little figures of horses, foxes, &c. &c. interspersed with stars, and many other similar devices.

The entire edifice is supported upon eight columns on either side: three constituting the chancel, and the remaining five the nave; the galleries are particularly neat, more especially that appropriated to the organ, the whole of the pewing being covered entirely with green baize, The lancet windows, with which the church was formerly furnished, have almost all been altered for others of a later date, except in the clerestory, where

they retain their original form..   The large
east window, before mentioned, was formerly adorned with no less than 14 coats of arms
richly painted.   The roof was put up, at the
time that the Norfolks were lords of the borough : in the year 1825, a curious old inscription was discovered upon the summit of
the walls, reaching from one end of the
church to the other, but it was very remarkable, that the centres of all the letters,
(which   were abouta footin length) were entirely, and apparently designedly effaced, so
that not the slightest meaning could be discovered from it.

In the chancel, is the curious and remar-
kable effigy of Thomas lord Braose ob. 1396.
This noble and ancient family were formerly
almost the sole proprietors of the county of
Sussex.   One of their residences was at
Chesworth, an ancient mansion   to   the

south of the town, which shall afterwards be
described ; and Bramber Castle also near
Steyning, originally appertained to these
powerful barons,   The head of the figure,

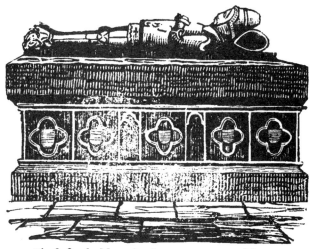

"is defended by a basinet, ornamented by a
draplet of jewels, his throat by the ample
carmail, attached to the helmet as in the time
of Edward III.   His arms are in plate ar-

mour, and his body in a shortened hauberk,
kept from pressing on his chest, by means of
the plastron, or breast-plate, within.   Over
this is the juppon, bearing his coat of arms,
viz. sem of cross croslets, a lion rampant
crowned.   Suspended from his military gir-
dle at his right hip, is his dagger, the sheath
of which, is ornamented in an architectural
style, and in the same manner at the left,
hung his long sword, of which no traces now
remain.   On his insteps, are large pieces attached to the spur leathers, and terminated
by indented edges which conceal the chain
mail beneath.   His jousting helmet, surmounted by his crest, a demi-lion rampant,
issuing from a coronet, is under his head,
but greatly mutilated, all below the oculari-
um, having been destroyed.*"

* Dallaway page 855 vol 2.

At a very small distance from the above
mentioned monument, is a very beautiful
altar tomb of white marble, relieved alter-
nately by slabs of black : upon this is an ad-
mirable and most elaborately executed fi -
gure, of a lady, in long flowing robes, her
right hand reclines upon her breast, while
her left rests upon the Holy Scriptures, in a
peculiarly graceful manner : it is the work
of Francis Fanelli, an Italian sculptor, of
great eminence in his day, and has escaped
the devastation generally inflicted on works
of art in the parochial edifices of Sussex; the
inscription is as follows.

Here lyeth (expecting a ioyfull resurction,) the body of
Elizabeth, late wife of Thom is Delves Esquire, son and
naire apparent to Sr. Henry Delves of Dvd lington in the
County of Chester, Barronet, who loe assed the 21 l day
of December 1654, being so newhat more than 25 yeares
old ; then in childbed of Henry their 2nd son, who with
Thomas their eldest son did both survive her. She was
enriched with many ornaments, both of mind and body,
and memorable for virtue, in the several relations of her
life, whereunto she was any way engaged. being religious
as she was a Christian, dutiful as a daughter, affectionate
as a wife .tender as a mother, discreete in her family a

a M stris, charitable in the relation of a neighbour, also
of a sweet and affable disposition and of a sober and win
nin conversation She was the only chid of Hall RaVens
croft Esq.r of this parish, by the mother descended ofye
Stapl ys of this ounty. Her sorrowful husband, sadley
weighing such a considerable losse, erected this monument, that an impartiall memeriel of her might bee the
better communicated to posterity.

On the south side, are the arms of the de-
ceased with the motto "In Dieu ma foy"

On the other side of the church, in a portion denominated the Rofly chancel, is a
large, and beautifully sculptured altar-tomb,

of Sussex marble, with a light and curious canopy of the same material, supported up-on pillars : on the surface were formerly a

brass inscription, and armorial bearings, but all of these have disappeared, it is supposed to cover the remains of Thomas Hoo Knt.

lord Hoo and de Hastings, ob. 1455.

According to Dallaway, mention is made in the visitation book of Philpot and Owen, A.D. 1634, of two other monuments, not at present remaining. "Under the communion table,

> 𝕳𝖎𝖈 𝖏𝖆𝖈𝖊𝖙 𝖂𝖎𝖑𝖑𝖎𝖆𝖒 𝕳𝖔𝖔 𝖆𝖗𝖒𝖎𝖌𝖊𝖗, 𝖖𝖚𝖎 𝖔-
> 𝖇𝖎𝖎𝖙 2𝖉𝖔 𝖒𝖊𝖓𝖘𝖎𝖘 𝕾𝖊𝖕𝖙, 1465

Arms, Hoo impaling a fess.

On a marble stone,

> 𝕲𝖗𝖆𝖙𝖊 𝖕𝖗𝖔 𝖆𝖓𝖎𝖒𝖆𝖇, 𝕿𝖍𝖔𝖒𝖆𝖊 𝕮𝖔𝖇𝖊𝖗𝖙 𝖊𝖙 𝖊𝖏𝖚𝖘
> 𝖚𝖗𝖔𝖗 𝖖𝖚𝖎 𝖖𝖓𝖎𝖉𝖊𝖒 𝕿𝖍𝖔, 𝖔𝖇, 1495,

Arms, two shields, 1 Covert, impaling a pha-on's head : 2 impaling, a chevron, 2 round-lets, in chief a buck's head caboshed."

Under the organ gallery, is a curious brass of a man and woman, in the antique dress of the time, with the following inscrip-

BRASS FIGURE.

tion, in Gothic characters, below them.

𝕳𝖊𝖗𝖊 𝖑𝖞𝖊𝖙𝖍 𝕽𝖎𝖈𝖍𝖆𝖗𝖉 𝕱𝖔𝖝𝖘, 𝖆𝖚𝖉 𝕰𝖑𝖎𝖟𝖎𝖇𝖊𝖙𝖍 𝖍𝖎𝖘 𝖜𝖎𝖋𝖊; 𝖜𝖍𝖎𝖈𝖍 𝕽𝖎𝖊𝖍𝖆𝖗𝖉 𝖉𝖊𝖈𝖊𝖆𝖘𝖊𝖉 𝖙𝖍𝖊 21 𝖉𝖆𝖞 𝖔𝖋 𝕬𝖕𝖗𝖎𝖑, 𝕸𝕯𝕷𝖄𝕴𝕴𝕴,

Affixed to one of the columns supporting the organ gallery, is a small slab of white marble, with a frame of black : the inscription in black letter runs thus.

In this seat is interred the body of
Thomas Pyke Barber and Chyrur-
geon, who departed this life the 16
day of Nov., in the year of our
Lord MDLXXXI; and in remem-
brance of him, this monument was
erected by his brother Wm. Pyke.

At a very small distance from this tablet, the

annexed inscription can be discovered upon
a stone in the middle cross aisle.

Here lyeth Robert Hvlsf of Hvrst hill, who died i. p.
1483, Nicholas his son, A.D. 1533, and Richard son ot
Nicholas Feb. 16th A.D. 1592.

The other monumental inscriptions are to
the following persons.

John Mitchell of Stammerham 1610, Mary
his wife daughter of William Gresham gent.
of Surrey, 1610; Maurice Barrow gent. 1778;
John Parsons esq. 1702; Cecilia Maria his
wife 1700; Mrs. Olive Eversfield, only sisters
to Mary wife of Charles Eversfield, of Denne
place, 1704 ; Rev. Geo. Marshall, 35 year
officiating minister of this parish, 1819;
Charles Eversfield of Denne place, and
Mary his wife; Sir Charles Eversfield Bart.,
1784; Mrs. Olive Eversfield 1803; Anna
Maria Willemot Thornton, 1824; William
Jamieson vicar of Horsham 1821 ; Edward
Tredcroft, 1768 ; Mary Tredcroft, 1794 ;

Sarah and Henry Du Cane Cap. Richard
Marriott, 1805, the beautiful female figure
which surmounts this monument, is the work

of Westmacot, Tristram Revel, lieut. col.
1797; Rev. T. White 1788; Thomas Brien
sen. 1741; Mrs Mary Jenden 1802; John
Smith esq. 1758; Elizabeth Smith; 1780;
Griffith Smith 1663; Charles Smith 1689;
Adam Smith 1789; Harriet Smith 1800:

Mrs Martha Longhurst 1750 ; John Foster
1750 ; Elizabeth Foster his wife 1743; John
Medwin eldest son of John Charles & Mary
Medwin, unfortunately killed by a fall from
a gig, at the foot of Picts hill near Horsham,
1806 ; Lieu. Henry Clough Medwin 1815 ;
Henry Ellis 1785 ; Mrs Ann Godwin 1822 ;
George Cheynell 1747 ; Elizabeth his wife,
1781 ; John Eversfield esq. 1669.   Besides
these there are slabs to the memory of the
following individuals. ---- Thomas Waller :
Thomas Dunball : Mary Woodyear : Willi-
am Norman : John Higgen : Thomas Buen:
Henry Waller :   John Rowland : Hannah
Howes : Ann Curtis : John Pilfold : Robert
Hall : William White : William Griffith :
Henry Griffith: Ann Griffith: Hen. Groom-
bridge : Elizabeth Hewet : Henry Ellis :
Henry Groombridge : Judith Jeamison :
Samuel, Sarah, and Catherine, Wicker :

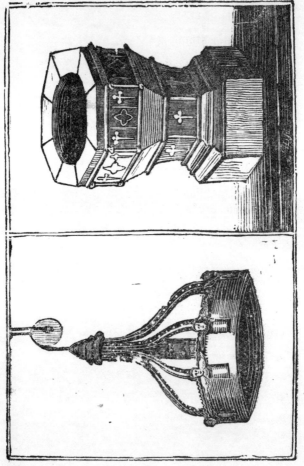

FONT AND COVER.

Matthew White: Francis Read: James
Waller: John Middleton esq.: Ann Chourn
Isabella Ramsden; Sir Bysshe Shelley Bart.
of Castle Goring: Mary Catherina his wife:
Catherine their daughter. All of these monuments, with the exception of six, belong
to the last century.

The font constructed of Sussex marble, is
octagonal, and handsomely sculptured: date
1455.

The following inscriptions are noticed in
the Burrel MSS. (British Museum,) which
at present do not remain.

In mortem Georgii Allen.

'Quod fuit esse, quod est, quod non fuit esse, quod esse,
Esse quod est, non esse quod est, non est erit esse:
Vita malis plena est, pia mors pretiosa corona est;
Post vitam mors est, post mortem vita beata est.

In the window of the North chancel, was
the following, in Gothic characters.

𝕺𝖗𝖆𝖙𝖊 𝖕𝖗𝖔 𝖆𝖓𝖎𝖒𝖆, 𝖂𝖎𝖑𝖎𝖊𝖒𝖎 𝕬𝖙𝖙𝖜𝖔𝖔𝖉 𝖉𝖊
𝕳𝖔𝖗𝖘𝖍𝖆𝖒 𝖊𝖙 𝕬𝖑𝖎𝖈𝖎𝖆 𝖚𝖗𝖔𝖗 𝖊𝖏𝖚𝖘, 𝖖𝖚𝖆 𝖎𝖘𝖙𝖆𝖒 𝖋𝖊-
𝖓𝖊𝖘𝖙𝖗𝖆𝖒 𝖋𝖎𝖊𝖗𝖎 𝖋𝖊𝖈𝖎𝖙 ;𝕬.𝕯. 1428.

"Madam Eversfield (according to Dallaway) gave one silver flaggon, two silver cups,
one basin for oblation, gilt ; pulpit cushion
and cloth, with gold fringe, and a branch of
candlesticks to the body of the church. Two
dozen of penny loaves, to be disp osed of a-
mong the poor every Sunday, that frequent
the church, for ever ; the gift of Mr Theobald Shelley." "The same person with the
Lady Matthews, gave this portion of bread
to be disposed of every Sunday for ever, for
the encouragement of the poor to frequent
the church." This is inscribed in front of the
organ gallery. In the parish registers mention is made of an attack of the plague, by
which this place was afflicted, though hap-
pily not to a very alarming extent, they com-

mence in the year 1560.   Over the vestry,
(which was built in the reign of Edward VI)
is a very curious old room reached by means
of a spiral stair-case, terminated by a trap
door : the oaken roof depends entirely upon
a large beam in the centre.   It is called the
Lollard's tower, and was most probably used
as a place of confinement   for that unfortunate sect : the apertures for light are thickly
guarded by double iron bars, and in one
place, on the north wall, the remains of an i-
ron ring are visible : the only thing of any
consequence in this cold and cheerless a-
partment, is a large oaken chest, curiously
carved, with a secret drawer of superior
workmanship. The beautiful service of communion plate is also kept here.

In the Roffy chancel is the beautiful monument of Mr Jamieson ; the figure of the
angel above, pointing upwards, is exquisite-

ly sculptured, and deserves much attention.

Dallaway mentions that there appear to have been two chantries and a brotherhood founded in this church, whose history is rather obscure, in some measure contradictory; the first he adds, "was built by Walter Burgess who in the year 1307, obtained a license to endow with 50 acres of land, a chaplain to celebrate divine service daily in the parish church of Horsham, for the souls of himself and his successors. The other was denomi-

mated Butler's chantry, and was founded by
one John Body and others by the lycens of
King Hen. VI, for one chapleyn to say dili-
gent service for ever, as th'aulter of St Mi-
chauel in the church of Horsham ; to pray
for the soulles of King Henry &c. ; the said
chapleyn to have for his wagis vij^{li} for the
year, for ever, which hath been continued
accordingly till about viij yeares past, at
which time Sir Will, Brandon, clerk, then
incumbent, sold the same unto Sir Roger
Copley, and after such sale by him made, he
the said Sir William, did sing after the
space vj yeares, and the said Sir Roger Coq-
ley paid him his wagis. ' " "Horsham, ----
Butler's Chantry.----- William Brandon of
th'age of ---- yeares, was last incumbent
there, but not resident, since anno reg. xxvij
who sold his interest to Mr Copley for viij ^{li}

xi s. ij d.*   At the west end of the building
is a large massy tower, lately put into tho-
rough repair, this is surmounted by an octagonal spire, 230 feet in height, and formed
of wooden shingles carefully fitted together.
The great bell of this church is the largest
in the county, and weighs nearly a ton and a
half : the whole peal, consisting of eight, is
extremely melodious.

On the 17th of November 1231, John de
Braose granted the church of Horsham with
all its appurtenances, to the prioress and
nuns of Rusper, for their exclusive use ; by
same deed it was also ordained, that on account of the size of the parish, and the number of inhabitants, the vicar who shall officiate in the church from time to time, shall

---

* Declaration of Chantries in the Augmentation office.

have one chaplain as his assistant, and two subordinate ministers, viz. a deacon and sub-deacon, to officiate with him in the same church.   At the dissolution of monastic establishments, in the reign of Henry VIII, the Archbishop of Canterbury came   into the patronage of the vicarage.

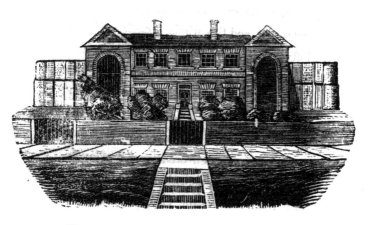

The county gaol is situated in East street, upon a very elevated site : it was erected about 50 years since, by William Griffith, who ruined himself, by contracting for the building : it is a neat and handsome structure, and extremely appropriate for the purpose, on the South is a smallgarden extendingalong the front of the building, which has two court-yards, of about half an acre each, with a gravel walk surrounding a fine grass-plot, and the whole is encircled by a lofty wall. To prevent confusion or danger in caseof fire, every cell is arched over with brick, and a separate room allotted to each debtor and felon. The chapel is in the keeper's house, where prayers are read daily, and a sermon delivered every Sunday by the chaplain. The annual salary of the keeper is 180 l. : that of the Chaplain 160 l. and of the Surgeon 70 l. per annum : the matron and the three male turnkeys receive 8s. each weekly : the internal management is regula-

ted by rules made at the quarter sessions,
and confirmed by the judges of assize.

The Independent's chapel, is situated
near the end of West Street, it is peculiarly
neat, both as respects its external and interior appearance: an inscription upon an o-
val tablet in front, informs us, that it was e-
rected by voluntary subscription in the year
1814.   At the distance of about a hundred
yards from the above, is the Roman Catholic chapel, with an embattled front surmoun-

ted by a cross: service is performed here, only once a fortnight; proceeding on in the same direction, we arrive at the Anabaptist chapel, a respectable building of some antiquity, a little to the left of which is the Friends' meeting house, in a very pretty retired situation.   The Wesleyan chapel was

erected in Brunswick place, A.D. 1832, it is simple in its style, but exceedingly neat, elegant, and appropriate: the last religious edifice in Horsham, is the Baptist's chapel, situated in New Street, it much resembles the Independant's in its exterior appearance.

"Richard Collier by his will dated Jan 23 1532, benevolently left a small estate, at Stratford le Bow in the county of Middlesex

to be sold, and the product to be laid out in the purchase of a school house at Horsham, where he was born."* The children enjoying the privileges of this charity, are annual-

* Dallaway.

ly selected by the vicar and churchwardens
with eight of the most "honest" inhabitants,
they are allowed to remain till the age of 14
and any number may at the discretion of the
school wardens, be instructed in the Latin
language.　It is expressly ordered in the
will, that the children elected, should be the
offspring of "poor people, in especial of the
said parish, and next about the same, to be
educated in reading, writing, arithmetic, and
the principles of the christian religion." The
charitable founder also bequeathed to the
Mercers' Company, a house and premises in
Cheapside London, for the support of the
master and usher, whose annual salaries are,
120 l. for the former, and 80 l. for the latter.
The school house is situated in a peculiarly
delightful and romantic situation, with a
pleasant croft in front, extending to the east
side of the church yard ; the accompanying

THE BRITISH SCHOOLS.

wood-cut represents the west front of the
building.

The National School is held in the church
porch, where great numbers of the younger
children of the poor are instructed.

A very neat building, denominated Denne
School, has been erected in a delightful situation, at the foot of the hill, from which it
takes its name, for the education of the girls
of the neigbouring indigent persons.

In the back lane, the members of the
church of England, have instituted an in-
fant school, which appears a very pleasant
object in this hitherto neglected portion of
the town.

The Royal British Schools are also well
worth the inspection of the visitor : the
boys are taught reading, writing, gram-
mar, linear and perspective drawing &c.

To the North of Horsham, on Hurst hill,

is Moated House, formerly belonging to the
family of the Westons: this mansion was the
residence of Robert Hurst ob. 1483, whose
monument in the church, the reader will re-
member,

Nearer the town, is a very ancient building formerly belonging to lord Hoo and de
Hastings, whose remains are interred in the
church: a farm house at present the property of the duke of Norfolk alone marks the
site of this once splendid and princely edifice.

Chesworth, one of the oldest houses in the
county, was formerly as before said, the residence of the noble family of Braose, this
truly romantic structure is situated a little
to the south east of the town, of which it is
one of the chief objects of interest. The
unfortunate Thomas duke of Norfolk, who
fell a victim to the malignant jealousy of

NORTH CHAPEL

CHESWORTH HOUSE.

Queen Elizabeth, was apprehended here,
A.D. 1571. It is said that the papers con-
cealed by Higford, and which led to his con-
viction, were discovered under the roof of
this building. Several apartments of very
spacious dimensions, but of whose existence
the inhabitants were totally ignorant, were
discovered through accident, by a maid servant about 20 years since. The chapel now
used as a wash-house, is still quite perfect, and of great height: several niches for
the statues of saints, and receptacles for holy water, may be discovered in the sides:
through the falling of part of the wall, a few
years ago, several Roman coins were dug
up, from which circumstance, it has been by
some persons imagined, that the place was
originally a Roman villa.

To the west of the town, is Hills place, or
rather the remains of an elegant residence,

so called ; it was formerly the property of
the lords Irvine, and was considered a very
handsome specimen of the domestic architecture of the age, in which it was erected.

[Hills place.1787.]

It was taken down a few years since, and no
vestige left to mark its site, save the remnants of a farm house in existence before the
building of the mansion itself, and part of a
wing added to the structure, on the marriage
of lord William Ingram, one of the family.

In one of the upper rooms, is a venerable escocheon, with the motto "In cœlo quies," serving to exclude the wind from the antique chamber.

On a lofty eminence denominated Denne hill, the visitor may obtain a very beautiful view of the town of Horsham, with its adjacent hills behind, the interesting church appears by far the most conspicuous object in the wide extended landscape, while the small and winding branch of the river Arun, which takes its rise in the adjacent forest of of St. Leonard, contributes not a little to heighten the beauty, and diversify the scene, of this truly delightful and extensive prospect.

At a short distance from the spot where this romantic view may be obtained, the ivied tower, and venerable battlements of Denne house, proudly rise upon the sight,

The spot upon which this edifice stands, is
particularly interesting, being generally supposed by antiquarians to be the site of a Da-
nish encampment, during a conflict with the
Picts, who made choice of an opposite eminence, still retaining the name of Pict's hill,
while the one we have just described pre-
serves the appellation of Denne (undoubted
ly derived from Dane) hill. The estate formerly belonging to the family of Braose,
was forfeited to the crown, with other lands,
on the attainder of Thomas duke of Norfolk
into whose possession it had fallen : in the
year 1594, it was awarded by Sir William
Covert and Sir John Caryll to James Boath,
by whom it was sold five years afterwards to
Stephen Barnham of London for 1250 l.
Shortly afterwards however the two sons of
the last mentioned person, parted with it to
Sir Thomas Eversfield for the sum of 5500 l.

DENNE HOUSE.

After passing through the hands of several of his descendants, it devolved to William Markwick esq, who took the name of Eversfield, and to whose grandson a minor it now belongs.

Continuing along the London road from

Warnham Church.

Horsham for about 3 miles, and then pursuing the road to the left, we arrive at the picturesque, secluded, and delightful little village of Warnham, bounded on the east by
Rusper, west by Slinfold, south by Itching-

Monument of Sir John Caryl

field, and north by Capel, and containing in
1831, 952 inhabitants. The village is rather
extensive, and consists principally of one
long narrow street, running N. and S. ; the
church on the west side is particularly neat,
though exhibiting a variety of style, and consists of a nave and south aisle, with three
chancels : the northern of these latter por-
tions is divided from the south aisle, by
a handsome oaken skreen, carved in the Gothic style, and formerly belonged to the Ca-
rylls. On the north side is a curious old
mural monument, bearing the effigies of a
man in armour and a woman kneeling ; below are 8 smaller figures intended for their
children, with another person armed, in the
centre. The inscription informs us that it
was erected to the memory of Sir John Caryll Knt., eldest son of Thomas Caryll esq.
of Warnham, and Maria his wife, daughter

of George Cotton of Warblington, ob. 1613.
The south chancel belonged to the Mitchell
family of Field Place, and contains monuments to the memory of Mary Mitchell widow, mother of Edward Shelley esq., by Sir
Timothy Shelley gent, ob. 1731 ; John
Mitchell gent. 1711: John Shelley esq. 1799;
Mary his wife 1759 : Edward Shelley esq, of
Field place 1747.   The centre chancel, formerly belonging to the appropriation, is at
present, in conjunction with the other two,
the property of Sir Timothy Shelley Bart.
In the body of the church are slabs to Samuel Shuckford, 45 years vicar of Warnham
and Eartham, Ann his widow, and Matthew
Napper gent.   In the pavement of the south
aisle, the side of an altar tomb, adorned with
shields and quatrefoils, and apparently of
the time of Edward I, may be discerned: the
font is square, and of the same date; the pul-

pit stands upon a basement of brick, which gives it a particularly singular appearance : the neat embattled tower contains five bells, and is of later construction than the rest of the building.

Warnham Court, a handsome mansion in

the style of Elizabeth, and a very striking feature of the surrounding country, was e-rected about three years since, by Henry Tredcroft esq. : the house contains about 50 apartments, and is built of brick faced with stone : the grounds are tastefully ar-ranged, and the park, though so recently

laid out, assumes a beautiful and verdant appearance.

To the south of Warnham, is Field Place,
the residence for several centuries of the family of Mitchell. The only daughter of the
Rev. Theobald Mitchell, married the late

Sir Bysshe Shelley, by whose son Sir Timothy, it is now possessed. Percy Bysshe
Shelley, the celebrated poet and friend of
Byron, was born here : a brief but interesting account of his life, may be found in

Horsefield's "History of Sussex," vol. 2nd.
under the description of Warnham.

To the east of Horsham, is a tract of land,
containing between eight and nine thousand
acres, called St. Leonard's forest : although
its nearest point is seven miles from the upper part of Beeding, it is within the limits of
that parish: the chief part of the soil is poor,
it contained considerable quantities of iron
stone, which was smelted, but as the timber
became exhausted, the smelting of the iron
has been long discontinued, and nothing remains to denote the former manufactory of
cast iron, but several large ponds in various
parts of the forest, still called Hammer
ponds.

This forest has ever been the subject of the
legends of neighbouring peasants, woe (according to their account) to the luckless
wight, who should venture to cross it alone

on horseback during the night, for no soon-
will he have entered its darksome precincts,
than a horrible decapitated spectre in the
shape of a former squire Paulett, disregard-
ing all prayers or menaces, leaps behind
him on his good steed, and accompanies the
affrighted traveller to the opposite bounda-
ries. --- The celebrated St. Leonard also,
through whose efficacious prayers

"The adders never stynge,
Nor ye nyghtyngales synge,"

in its gloomy mazes is often the theme of the
cottagers fire side conversation

But neither ghost, nor cast iron, nor saint
Leonard himself, have gained for this forest
so much celebrity as its famous DRAGON,
or serpent! This venemous reptile, which
some persons have rendered into some ob-
noxious proprietor, has been honoured with

a long and minute description in the following account.

"True and wonderful, A discourse relating to a
strange monstrous serpent or dragon, lately discovered, and yet living to the great annoyance
and divers slaughters both of men and cattle by
his strong and violent poyson, in St. Leonard's
forest, an d thirtie miles from London, this present month of August, 1614, with the true ge-
neration of serpents.   Printed at London by
John Trundle 1614.

In Sussex there is a pretty market towne,
called Horsam, neare unto a forest called St
Leonard's forest, and there in a vast unfre-
quented place, heathie, vaultie, full of un-
wholesome shades and overgrown hollowes,
where this serpent is thought to be bred;
but wheresoever bred, certaine and too true
it is, that there it yet lives.   Within three
or four miles compass are its usual haunts,
oftentimes at a place called Faygate, and it

hath been seene within half a mile of Horsam, a wondre no doubt most terrible and
noysome to the inhabitants thereabouts.
There is always in his tracke or path, left a
glutinous and slimy matter (as by a small si-
militude we may perceive in a snail) which
is very corrupt and offensive to the scent, in
so much that they perceive the air to be pu-
trified withall, which must needs be very
dangerous: for though the corruption of it
cannot strike the outward parts of a man,
unless heated into blood, yet by receiving it
in at any of our breathing organs, (the nose
or mouth) it is by authority of all authors
writing in that kinde, mortal and deadlie ;
as one thus saith,

'Noxia serpentum est admixto sanguine pestis.--LUCAN.'

The serpent, or dragon as some call it, is
reputed to be nine feete or rather more, in

length, and shaped almost in the forme of an
axle-tree of a cart, a quantitie of thickness
in the middest, and somewhat smaller at
both ends. The former part which he
shootes forth as a necke, is supposed to be
about an ell long, with a white ring as it
were of scales about it.   The scales along
his backe, seeme to be blackish, and so,
much as is discovered under his bellie, ap-
peareth to be red : for I speak but of no.
nearer description than a reasonable ocular
distance; for coming too neare, it hath al-
ready been too dearely paid for, as you shall
heare hereafter.   It is likewise discovered to,
have large feete, but the eye may be dece-
ved, for some, suppose that serpents have
no feete, but glide along upon certain ribbes,
and scales, which both defend them from,
the upper part of the throat unto the lower
part of their bellie, and also cause them to,

move much the faster.   For so this doth,
and rids away as we call it, as fast as a man
can run.   He is of countenance very proud,
and at the sight or heareing of men and cattle, will raise his necke upright, and seem to
listen and looke about with great arrogan-
cie. There are likewise on either side of him
discovered two great bunches, so big as a
large footeball, and as some think will grow
to wings, but God I hope will so defend the
poor people in the neigbourhood, that he
shall be destroyed, before he growe so
fledge. ---- He will cast his venome about 4
roddes from him, as by woeful experience
it was proved on the bodies of a man and woman coming that way, who afterwards were
found dead, being poysoned and very much
swelled, but not preyed upon.   Likewise a
man going to chase it and as he imagined to
destroy it with two mastiff dogs as yet not

knowing the great danger thereof, his dogs
were both killed, and he himself glad to re-
turne with haste to preserve his own life :
yet this is to be noted that the dogs were
not preyed upon, but slaine and left whole,
for his food is thought to be for the most
part in a conie warren, which he often fre-
quents, and it is found to be much scanted
and impaired, in the encrease it had wont to
afford. — These persons, whose names are
here under printed, have seene this serpent,
besides divers others, as the carrier of Horsam, who lieth at the White Horse, in
Southwark, and who can certifie the truth
of all that hath been herein related.-----

        "John Steele,

        "Christopher Holder,

    "And a widow woman dwelling at Fay-
gate."

Previously to the reformation, St. Leonard's forest contained two chapels, one of which is mentioned as early as the year 1320. No traces of either remain at the present day.

Proceeding from Horsham along the London road, and passing Thornton ville, a collection of houses lately erected by the person resident at Springfield, we arrive at Coolhurst, the delightful and elegant mansion of the Marchioness of Northampton : the vicinity of this seat was lately rendered particularly interesting by a romantic and beautiful glen called Dubbin's Green, one of the wildest and most secluded spots in the district, but it is greatly to be lamented, the enclosing of the adjacent common, has almost entirely destroyed the beauty of the scenery, and robbed the visitor of a

truly rural and picturesque treat. Continuing along the turnpike road for some distance, and then inclining to the right, the
pretty little village of Nuthurst, with its mo-

Nuthurst Church.

dest spire peeping amidst the lowly cottages

which constitute the single street is display-
before the sight.   To the east of the parish
is a portion of St. Leonard's forest, and a
part of the parish of Cowfold: to the west
Horsham, and part of Broadwater ; to the
north another portion of the forest; and
south Cowfold.   The district is peculiarly
rich and beautiful, abounding in springs of
excellent water in every direction.   The
church, of the time of Edward III, and dedicated to St. Andrew, is in the early style
of English architecture, with a low tower,
containing 3 bells, and surmounted by a low
shingled spire, at the west end.   The roof
is pannelled in a similar manner to the
church at Horsham ; the ribs and knots of
two pannels are gilt and painted.   The
communion window contains remnants of
stained   glass, representing the Salvator
Mundi, and two   angels   scattering in-

cense. The monumental inscriptions are to
the memory of Joseph Tuder esq. of
Sedgewick park, 1774 : Rebecca Nelthorpe
his niece, 1784; William Nelthorpe esq.,
1791 : Elizabeth Nelthorpe 1801 ; Eliza
Sarah wife of James Tuder Nelthorpe esq.
of Nuthurst lodge, died at Paris 1826, and
was interred in the cemetry of Pere la chaise
John Aldridge of New Lodge, 1803 : John
Warburton Aldridge son of the above, 1801:
Samuel Aldridge 1773 : Sophia Aldridge
1769. The font is plain and octagonal.

Near Nuthurst in a very delightful situation, commanding extensive views of the
sea and south downs, is Nuthurst Lodge'
the residence of James Tuder Nelthorpe
esq. : at a very short distance from the mansion, are the remains of an ancient castle or
hunting seat, surrounded by an oute

and inner moat, of a circula. form, and tra-
ceable every where ; the foundations of the
walls are quite visible, and one apartment of
a sexagonal shape is entirely perfect.   A-
bout 40 yards farther on, surrounded by
copse wood, and over hanging trees, is a
small well of a circular form, and surrounded,
by cut stone overgrown by moss : a flight of
winding steps, leading to it, from an adjacent eminence, adds a peculiarly romantic
and pleasing effect to this venerable work of
antiquity, which is known by the name of the
Nun's Well.   No account is to be found of
its history, though it may perhaps have belonged to the neighbouring castle.   The
traditions among the inhabitants affirm, that
that a subterraneous passage connects this
castle with the nunnery at Rusper, which is
8 miles distant, but no attempt has been un-
dert aken to ascertain the truth of this con-

jecture.   Passing over Tower Hill, an
eminence near Horsham, we arrive at the
village of Itchingfield, or Hethinfield as it
was formerly called.   The earliest notice of
this place, is to be found in an ancient deed
A.D. 1233, when "Hugh de Mabel and Su-
sanna his wife, sold to Robert atte Feching,
one messuage and half a carucate of land, at
Hethinfield."The parish is bounded on the
east by Horsham, south by Shipley, west by
Shipley, and north by Slinfold, and contained in 1831, 349 inhabitants.   The church
dedicated to St. Nicholas is of the time of
Henry III, or Edward the I.   Its exterior
is particularly rustic especially the low tower at the west end, which is formed of entire
trunks of trees fastened together by wooden
bolts.   Against one of the walls of timber
in the belfry is an ancient painting representing Moses receiving the ten command-

ments on mount Sinai, it was most probably used as a kind of altar piece.

Itchingfield Church.

In the chancel is a mural monument to the memory of Richard Wheatly gent, ob. 1668, and some members of his family, who were nearly allied to the Mitchells of Field place.

There is also another inscription to the me-
ory of the Rev. Alexander Hay, former rector of this parish, 1724, also several of his
children. Dallaway mentions that after the
Scotch rebellion in 1715, some of the attain-
tedpersons took refuge in the woods of Itch-
ing field, and were permitted to reside with
their countryman Alexander Hay; indeed
we can hardly imagine a more suitable place
for concealment, than the parsonage house,
situated as it was at that time, in the centre
of a dense forest, through which there was
hardly any passable road.

The last monumental inscription is for the
Rev. Thomas Lavender a most exemplary
minister of this parish, for upwards of 60
years, he died in the year 1776, at the age
of 86.

The font is modern, but particularly neat
and handsome; one of a very ancient des-

cription, was lately dug up in the church-
yard.

Proceeding along the turnpike road to
the west of Horsham and passing Farthing

Bridge, of which the annexed wood-cut is a
representation, we reach Broad-bridge
Heath, a delightful, picturesque, and salu-
brious plain, so called : by pursuing the
centre road, the visitor will arrive at Stroud,
a small hamlet about 3 miles from Horsham;
it is chiefly remarkable for the elegant resi-

dence denominated Stroud park, belonging
to ---- Commerell esq. : the grounds around
the house particularly deserve attention, and
the sweetly retired situation of the fishing
house, erected upon the banks of a lake surrounded by the majestic and noble trees for
which this district is so justly celebrated,
whilst the deep silence which pervades the
whole, interrupted only by the rippling
stream beneath, and the delightful choir of
the feathered songsters, combine to render
it, in every sense of the word, a most en-
chanting and delightful scene.

By taking the road to the left hand, on
Broad-bridge heath, and again turning to
the right at Lion's Corner gate, the village
of Slinfold, to which the hamlet of Stroud
belongs, soon appears in sight. "Fold" observes Mr. Dallaway, "is a termination fre-

quently belonging to parishes within the
weald and in distinction to Hu ᚠᚦᚳ seems to
be applied to those which were first cultiva-
ted in square inclosures, after the removal
of timber and underwood. This observa-
tion belongs to the early Saxon æra; and it

Slinfold Church

is evident that the name of almost every vil-
or farm within the district is derived from

them." The
church built at
theend of the vil-
lage, was erec-
ed at the forma-
t
tion of the parish
by bishop Ralph
in 1230. It has
a nave and north
aisle with a small
sepulchral chap-
el appendant. In
this portion of
the churchwhich
belongs to the
manor of Dedis-

ham, is a curiously sculptured female figure,

destitute of any inscription, but traditionally said, to belong to a member of the family of Tregoz.——There are also two other mural monuments, with small painted alabaster effigies of women in the ancient dress of their times. The first of which we give a sketch

appears particularly "en bon point," and is
represented kneeling on a cushion, in the
act of prayer. The following inscription,
now almost illegible, appears beneath

HERE LIETH KATHARINE BLOUNT, YOUNGEST DAUGHTER OF
RICHARD BLOUNT ESQ., OF DEDISHAM, (DESCENDED FROM
SIR WALTER BLOUNT KNT. LORD MOUNTJOY) AND MARY
WIFE TO THE SAID RICHARD, DAUGHTER TO SIR WILLIAM
WESTE, KNT., LORD DE LA WAR, WHICH KATHARINE DE-
CEASED MARCH 1, 1617, IN THE 27TH. YEAR OF HER AGE.
SHE LEFT HER ESTATE TO HER 4 SISTERS, VIZ. ELIZABETH,
ANN, MARTHA, AND JANE, TO WHOSE PIOUS MEMORY THEY
ERECTED THIS MONUMENT.

The remaining monument is to the memory of mistress Jane Blount, ob. 1614.

In the pavement is a large slab of Sussex
marble, with an inscription to the memory
of Richard Bradbridge gent., and Denys his
wife, with their children, ob. 1633.

The tower is massive, and like all those in
the Weald, surmounted by a spire of shin-

gles, supported upon four upright beams of
a length and diameter very seldom seen:

This parish which is bounded on the east
by Warnham, west by Rudgewick and Bil-
linghurst, north by Rudgewick, and south
by Itchingfield, approaches nearer in form
to a circle than any other, and is intersected
in several directions by 3 turnpike roads.
From the excellent slate quarries in the vicinity, slabs containing 100 square feet, and
about 5 in thickness have often been raised.
Several rare botanical plants are found in
this parish, some indigenous, and others o-
riginally introduced by Dr. T. Manningham
a former rector, well versed in that science.

The late eminent antiquary Mr. Warton,
observes in his history of Kiddington, page
65, "About 5 years ago, (1775) on the edge
of a lane in the parish of Slinfold in Sussex,
four miles from Horsham, I saw several deep

fissures in the Stane street, a Roman road,
going from Arundel, if not from the sea side
through Dorking to London.   The dorsum
not intended for heavy carriages consists of
sea gravel and sea pebbles abounding on the
Sussex coast, above 3 feet deep, and 7 yards
long: these minute materials must have been
amassed with prodigious labour.

Springfield, a handsome brick mansion to
the north of the town, is the property of
Francis Scawen Blunt esq., who now rents it
to —— Thornton esq.

INNS AT HORSHAM

The King's Head Hotel . . . . . . East Street.
Anchor Hotel . . . . Town Hall square.
The Crown . . . . Carfax.
The Lamb . . . . Ditto.
The Swan . . . . West Street.
The Castle . . . . Ditto.
The Black Horse. . . . . Ditto.
The Punch bowl . . . . Ditto.
The Green Dragon . . . . Bishoprick.
The Queen's Head . . . . , . . . East Street.
The Hurst Arms. . . . . North Street.
The Dog and Bacon . . . . London Road.
The White Hart . . . . North Parade.

COACHES.

Coaches pass daily to and from London, Brighton, Worthing, Windsor, Oxford, and Reading.—The Horsham and London Star Coach leaves the Swan inn West Street, at 7 o'clock every morning, and reaches the old Bell inn Holborn about a quarter to 12 : from thence it starts the same afternoon, at a quarter past 3, and arrives at Horsham by 8.

GAS.

The streets are now well lighted with gas, considering that this is the first year of their illumination. The ga-

MAP OF THE COUNTRY

Four Miles around Horsham 1835.

meter is erected at the back of Albion Terrace, another specimen of the improving state of the town. The good people of Horsham have lately been much annoyed by the dirty condition of their streets, occasioned by the insertion of the gas pipes, even to such an extent as almost to merit the ancient epithet of the county, as we find in a very old verse, or rather ryhme of the peculiarities of each shire.

> Essex ful of good hoswifes
> Middlesex ful of shyves,
> Kentshire hoot as fyre,
> Sussex ful of dyrt and myre.

PLANTS.

RHYNCHOSPORA ALBA
SCIRPUS CARINATUS
ERYOPHORUM POLY-
  STACHION
CONVALLARIA MAJA-
  LIS
LUCIOLA FOSTERI
POLYGONUM BISTOR-
  TA
ADOXA MOSCHATELLI-
  NA
MONOTROPA HYPOPI-
  TYS
PYROLA MEDIA
NYMPHÆA ALBA
CARDAMINE IMPATI-
  ENS
EUPHORBIA ESULA
CAREX CURTA
CAREX STRIGOSA

ASPIDIUM CREOPTE-
  RIS
ASPIDIUM THELYPTE-
  RIS
OSMUNDA REGALIS
LYCOPODIUM SELAGO
PHASCUM ALTERNI-
  FOLIUM
GYMNOSTOMUM FAS-
  CICULARE
NECKERA PUMILA
CALICIUM FERRUGI-
  NEUM
ARTHONIA SWARTZIA-
  NA
VARIOLARIA VELATA
PARMELIA SPECIOSA
SCYPHOPHORUS PARA-
  SITICUS
CHARA GRACITIS

SAURIAN REMAINS

The strata around Horsham, (which is situated in the Wealden formation) are celebrated for the abundance of the exuviæ, of large saurian animals. —— Many of the bones of the Iguanadon, an enormous reptile, which was formerly an inhabitant of these districts, are now in the possession of Mr G. B. Holmes, of Horsham, by whom these particulars are obligingly communicated. The animal which more nearly approximates to it, than any other now in existence, is the Iguana Cornuta a native of the tropical parts of America, and from its resemblance to which it has received its name ; but more particularly on account of the teeth of the Iguanadon, which resemble those of no other animal than the Iguana, of which one species (the Cornuta,) has, like the Iguanadon, a single horn. If we take the Iguana as our model, and attempt to reconstruct the enormous Iguanadon in just proportion, from the relics which have been frequently exhumed, we shall produce a monster 100 feet in length, which there is every reason to believe is not an exaggeration.——Besides the Iguanadon, we find the bones of the crocodile, the Plesiosaurus, the turtle, and other amphibious reptiles ; with the carbonized remains of monocotyledoneous plants, arborescent ferns, and palms,& c.

WATER.

The water around Horsham is of a very superior quality, and extremely abundant. It is intended shortly to sup-

ply each house by means of pipes. At **Tower Hill, is a**
spring, by whose waters every thing over **which it passes**
is encrusted, in consequence of its depositing **a small por.**
tion of carbonate of lime, with which it is impregnated in
passing the limestone strata, through which it flows.

POPULATION

The population of Horsham, has of late years greatly
encreased, and at present amounts to nearly 600,0.   **The**
following table will afford a view of its advance during the
present century.

1801	.	.	.	.	3204
1811	.	.	.	.	3839
1821	.	.	.	.	4575
1831	.	.	.	.	5105

ROADS.

Horsham, though at present remarkable for the excellent
state of its turnpike roads was, before the year 1750, one of
most extraordinary instances of non communication in t e
kingdom: previously to the abovementioned period, the
London road was so execrably bad, that whoever went
there on wheels, was compelled to go round by Canterbury !

It is intended to make the great London and Brighton
rail road pass through the town, which cannot fail to encreas
the business and traffic of the place.

FAIRS.

The fairs of Horsham are on April 5th: Monday before
Whitsunday; sheep and lambs: July 18th cattle and ped..
lary ; the Cherry fair; Sep. 5th. cattle: Nov. 27th. cattle
and toys. Last Tuesday in every month, for cattle

"Nicholas Hostresham, whose name is
contracted to Horsham, may justly be placed
in this town, as descended from it ; families
of note often taking their names from their
places of residence ; and if that be admitted,
he will give some lustre to it, for he was a very learned man, and so famous a physician,
that the nobility coveted his company on a-
ny conditions, so high an esteem had they
for him. It seems it was something of a pe-
culiar art in him, to cure and yet to please
his patient, which he would not do nevertheless it was consistent with the disease ; for
his aim was, to cure and please if possible,
but displease if unavoidable. He was of a
a middle temper, neither so rough as to af-

fright, nor so gentle, as to humour his patient into his own destruction; so that he was
almost two physicians in one man.   He died
in the year 1448. "

(From a survey of the county of Sussex,
printed in the year 1730; at present in the
possession of Miss Cove, Albion Terrace.)

APPENDIX.

══◦══

Having principally confined the limits of the foregoing account, to a circle of about 4 or 5 miles around the town of Horsham, we have omitted previously to notice the priory of Rusper, a building of great antiquity, and closely connected with that borough, by the endowment of the church to its nuns. Very little of the ancient edifice remains at present, I shall therefore insert a very brief account of the nunnery, as given by Sir William Burrell, in his interesting MSS. preserved in the British Museum.

"On the north wing of the east front of the nunnery, towards the orchard, the foundations of additional building, and the arch of a cellar are visible, 58 feet in extent, and east of the present house. It is probable a similar wing was on the south aspect and thereby formed a Greek II. The ancient apple trees which cover the flank, render such an idea very problematical." Near the building is a very deep well, said to have been used as a place of destruction for those members of the convent, who had dared to break their vows of chastity.

Near Mrs Delves tomb at Horsham, is the headless brass figure of an ecclesiastic, supposed from the letters 𝕿 𝕮 in the cope, to cover the remains of Thomas clerk, a former rector.

RUSPER NUNNERY.

BRASS FIGURE.

INDEX.

Printed by Howard Dudley, Millbank St.

PUBLISHER'S LIST

Facsimile
BLACK'S 1861 GUIDE TO SUSSEX
Incorporating 1859 Breads's guide to Worthing and a
description of the Miller's Tomb on Highdown Hill

This forms part of the South-Eastern Counties of England
series and comprises 184 pages. There is a folding map of
the county and steel engravings of the chain pier at Brighton,
Hastings and Chichester cathedral. Major towns are covered
as well as the smaller villages.

210 x 148mm 276 pages Engravings and folding map
ISBN 1 898941 21 1
Paperback **£8.95**
Hardback (cloth with gilt blocking to the front board and spine).
Limited edition 50 copies. **£25.00.**
Hardback (leather with gilt blocking to the front board and spine, mar-
bled endpapers, ribbon marker, in a matching cloth slipcase). Limited
edition of 100 copies. **£80.00.**

Facsimile
SHEPHERDS OF SUSSEX
Barclay Wills

Written as the last shepherds were disappearing from the
rural scene, with notes on Michael Bland, John Dudeney, etc.
Foreword by the Duke of Norfolk. The hill shepherd; lure of
the shepherd's work; a character study of Sussex shepherds;
shepherds of bygone days; the shepherd's possessions;
crooks & bells; shearing; sheep washing, marking & watering;
dew-ponds; Sussex sheep; the crow-scarer, etc.

185 x 125mm 280 pages 28 B&W photos
Hardback ISBN 1 898941 60 2 Price **£20.00**
Paperback ISBN 1 898941 67 X Price **£8.95**

Facsimile
SMUGGLING AND SMUGGLERS IN SUSSEX
'A gentleman of Chichester'

The genuine history of the inhuman and unparalleled murders of Mr William Galley, a customs house officer, and Mr Daniel Chater, a shoemaker, fourteen notorious smugglers, with the trials and execution of seven of the criminals at Chichester 1748-9.

Trials of John Mills and Henry Sheerman; with an account of the wicked lives of the said Henry Sheerman, Lawrence and Thomas Kemp, Richard Fuller and Jockey Brown; and the trials at large of Thomas Kingsmill and other smugglers for breaking open the Custom House at Poole, with the sermon preached in the Cathedral Church at Chichester, at a special Assize held there, by Bishop Ashburnham; also an article on 'Smuggling in Sussex' by William Durrant Cooper, Esq., FSA (reprinted from volume X of the Sussex Archaeological Collections) and other papers.

Hardback 185 x 125mm 280 pages Engravings
ISBN 1 898941 61 0
Price **£20.00**

FROM SUSSEX YEOMEN
TO GREENWICH WATERMEN
A W Gearing

Sussex 1500 - 1795. Greenwich 1795-1821. Greenwich 1821-1844. Greenwich 1844-1884. Greenwich 1884-1914. The Great War 1914-1922. Childhood memories 1922-1939. The war years 1939-1947. 1947-1985. Folkestone 1985-1997. Family tree.

Paperback 210 x 148mm 176 pages. Over 100 B&W photos
ISBN 1 898941 55 6
Price **£10.00**

A FULL LIFE IN DITCHLING, HASSOCKS AND BURGESS HILL 1919-1997
John Stenning

Ditchling, Sussex, between the wars. The farms, people & shopkeepers. Surrounding villages & towns.

Paperback 210 x 148mm 128 pages over 100 B&W photos
ISBN 1 898941 10 6
Price **£5.95**

A COUNTRYMAN'S FURTHER REMINISCENCES OF MID-SUSSEX
John Stenning

The South Downs · Farms & Farm folk · Early Days · Law-abiding men · Ditchling Folk · Dumbrell's School · Ditchling's Small Shops & Businesses · The Station Buses · Keymer & Hassocks · Sussanah Stacey of Stanton's Farm · Pouchlands Hospital · Streat & Westmeston · Ditchling Pageant · A Soldier's Diary

Paperback 210 x 148mm
160 pages over 100 B&W and 16 colour photos
ISBN 1 898941 42 4 Price **£7.50**

THE LIFE OF A MAN: RON SPICER 1929-1996
Dick Richardson & Doris Spicer

Ron Spicer was a herdsman at West Hoathly and a much-loved folk singer. This memoir includes reminiscences from those who knew him, songs from the repertoire and pictures from the family album. Foreword by Baroness Trumpington.

Paperback 200 x 210mm
64 pages B&W photos
ISBN 1 898941 06 8 Price **£6.50**

A DICTIONARY OF THE SUSSEX DIALECT
Rev WD PARISH
Edited by Dick Richardson

The dictionary was first published in 1875 by the vicar of Selmeston, the Rev WD Parish, following the pioneering work by Durrant Cooper. He also recorded provincialisms in use in the county at that time.

This new edition is augmented by further pieces on the Sussex dialect, traditional recipes, and a mumming play from West Wittering from the writings of EV Lucas, who died in 1938. (Highways & Byways in Sussex published by Macmillan & co, 1904. A facsimile edition of this will be published by Country Books in 2002.) Illustrated throughout with line drawings of Sussex views made in the late 19th and early 20th centuries by Frederick L Griggs, ARA.

Paperback 220 x 150mm 192 pages 70 line drawings
ISBN 1 898941 68 8 Price **£7.50**

**All books are available from good bookshops,
or in case of difficulty, from the publisher, post free.**

WRITING A BOOK?
Country Books is a small, independent publisher and has over 40 years publishing experience. In addition to our publishing activities, we undertake to produce books for other small publishers, individuals and societies (including the National Trust, Chatsworth House and Derbyshire County Council). This service began some years ago when we were submitted manuscripts which we felt worthy of publication but which, for one reason or another (usually because the likely print-run was too small to make it commercially viable), we were reluctant to take on under our own imprint. We would be pleased to assist you with the publication of your book.

Please contact us for further information:
COUNTRY BOOKS
Courtyard Cottage, Little Longstone, Bakewell, Derbyshire DE45 1NN
Tel/Fax: 01629 640670
e-mail: dickrichardson @ country-books.co.uk